the nerve of it

poems new and selected

lynn emanuel

pitt poetry series ed ochester, editor

the nerve of it

poems new and selected

lynn emanuel

university of pittsburgh press

Published by the University of Pittsburgh Press, Pittsburgh, Pa., 15260
Copyright © 2015, Lynn Emanuel
Manufactured in the United States of America
Printed on acid-free paper
10 9 8 7 6 5 4 3 2 1

ISBN 13: 978-0-8229-6369-1
ISBN 10: 0-8229-6369-8

Dear Maggie,
     There are no words for it.

Contents

III.

IV.

V.

Note To the Reader

Collections of new and selected poems are often arranged chronologically. As much as any other book of poems, a book of new and selected poems deserves its own distinctive shape. Chronology is predictable.

Muriel Rukeyser writes that poems in a book proceed either by linkage or collision. Here, I have used both. I have linked poems from different books and periods, and I have also arranged a series of collisions among some of them. I have ignored chronology, placing new poems beside old, mixing middle and early poems with recent work, and liberating all my poems from the restraints of their particular histories, both aesthetic and autobiographical. I hope you will read this as though I have, in fact, composed a new book.

Reading is entering
—Anne Blonstein

Out of Metropolis

We're headed for empty-headedness,
the featureless amnesias of Idaho, Nebraska, Nevada,
states rich only in vowel sounds and alliteration;
we're taking the train so we can see into the heart
of the heart of America framed in the windows' cool
oblongs of light. We want cottages, farmhouses
with peaked roofs leashed by wood smoke to the clouds;
we want the golden broth of sunlight ladled over
ponds and meadows. We've never seen a meadow.
Now, we want to wade into one—up to our chins in the grassy
welter—the long reach of our vision grabbing up great
handfuls and armloads of scenery at the clouds'
white sale, at the bargain basement giveaway
of clods and scat and cow pies. We want to feel half
of America to the left of us and half to the right, ourselves
like a spine dividing the book in two, ourselves holding
the whole great story together.

Then, suddenly, the train pulls into the station,
and the scenery begins to creep forward—the ramshackle shapes
of Main Street, a Chevy dozing at a ribbon of curb, and here is a hound
and a trolley, the street lights on their long stems, here is the little park
and the park stuff: idler on a bench, deciduous trees, a woman upholstered
in a red dress, the bus out of town sunk to its chromium bumper in shadows.
The noise of a train gathers momentum and disappears into the distance,
and there is a name strolling across the landscape in the crisply voluminous
script of the opening credits, as though it were a signature on the contract, as though
it were the author of this story.

Stone Soup

She wants to get born, so she invents a mother
to hold the long wooden wand of a cooking
spoon fast in her fist, the big black zero
of the iron pot, the stone of the pig's knuckle,
the buzz of the fridge, the tap scalding the soap
into suds, the tureen dunked, again, again;
she invents the tintinnabulation of the milkman's
bottles in their wire basket and the sigh
of the clutch as he disappears and the match
that touches the gas burner—the blue root,
the little tiara of yellow fire. Beyond the window
it is nearly dark, a sudsy ocean is coughing up
a beach as gray and hard as poured concrete.
She has set herself a task, like a train lugging
its hard body toward Portland, so she now makes
a father's coat come home from the day shift,
its pockets drooping like the jowls of a hound,
and his long black shoes with their dew of glitter
under the fluorescent light of the breakfast nook,
his mustache like a school janitor's brooms;
she begins with talk of labor and wages,
his big hand turning over the leaves of the light
and water bills like a boring book;
it will not be long now until she will make them
make her from nothing, a stone, a pot.

The Planet Krypton

Outside the window the McGill smelter
sent a red dust down on the smoking yards of copper,
on the railroad tracks' frayed ends disappearing
into the congestion of the afternoon. Ely lay dull

and scuffed; a miner's boot toe worn away and dim,
while my mother knelt before the Philco to coax
the detonation from the static. From Las Vegas
Tonapah Artillery and Gunnery Range the sound

of the atom bomb came biting like a swarm
of bees. We sat in the hot Nevada dark, delighted,
when the switch was tripped and the bomb hoisted
up its silky, hooded, glittering, uncoiling length;

it hissed and spit, it sizzled like a poker in a toddy.
The bomb was no mind and all body; it sent a fire
of static down the spine. In the dark it glowed like the coils
of an electric stove. It stripped every leaf from every

branch until a willow by a creek was a bouquet
of switches resinous, naked, flexible, and fine.
Bathed in the light of KDWN, Las Vegas,
my crouched mother looked radioactive, swampy,

glaucous, like something from the Planet Krypton.
In the suave brilliant wattage of the bomb, we were
not poor. In the atom's fizz and pop we heard possibility
uncorked. Taffeta wraps whispered on davenports.

A new planet bloomed above us; in its light
the stumps of cut pine gleamed like dinner plates.
The world was beginning all over again, fresh and hot;
we could have anything we wanted.

5

The Sleeping

I have imagined all this:
In 1940 my parents were in love
And living in the loft on West 10th
Above Mark Rothko who painted cabbage roses
On their bedroom walls the night they got married.

I can guess why he did it.
My mother's hair was the color of yellow apples
And she wore a velvet hat with her pajamas.

I was not born yet. I was remote as starlight.
It is hard for me to imagine that
My parents made love in a roomful of roses
And I wasn't there.

But now I am. My mother is blushing.
This is the wonderful thing about art.
It can bring back the dead. It can wake the sleeping
As it might have late that night
When my father and mother made love above Rothko
Who lay in the dark thinking *Roses, Roses, Roses.*

Of Your Father's Indiscretions and the Train to California

One summer he stole the jade buttons
Sewn down Aunt Ora's dress
And you, who loved that trail of noise and darkness
Hauling itself across the horizon,
Moths spiraling in the big lamps,
Loved the oily couplings and the women's round hats
Haunting all the windows
And the way he held you on his knee like a ventriloquist
Discussing the lush push of grass against the tree's roots
Or a certain crookedness in the trunk.
Now everything is clearer.
Now when the train pulls away from the station
And the landscape begins to come around, distant and yet familiar,
That odd crease of yellow light
Or the woods' vague sweep framed in the window forever
Remind you of the year you were locked up at the Hotel Fiesta
While father went out with fast black minks.
And how wonderful it was
When he was narrow as a hat pin in his tux
And to have come all that way on his good looks.
How wonderful to have discovered lust
And know that one day you would be on its agenda
Like the woman who drank and walked naked through the house
In her black hat, the one you used to watch
Through a stammer in the drapes.
In that small town of cold hotels, you were the girl in the dress,
Red as a house burning down.

Lunch Break with Ted Berrigan and Neighbor's House on Fire

It's 12 P.M. in the dark neighborhoods of sad youth.
Ouch, Burning House, when are you going out?
Red windows shut your red mouths. I cannot endure
Your hot voices swarming through me because now
In my poem I have become you! I thought,
"I put this house in my poem and I can take it out."
Ted, I thought this burning house was something
I could don and doff. Is this what art feels like?
And what it feels like to be (in) art? On fire not able to stop?
Shut up, you red ambulance, a poet is inside you!
At heart we are infinite, we are ethereal, we are weird!
And yet, Dear Ted, forgive me, but I need the boat of a bigger name:
Four syllables—*Odysseus*—myself tied to the mast of it
Listening to the sirens scream.

Drawing Rosie's Train Trip

I begin with the tree's left foot,
the long, black, raw, wet root

stubbing a toe in the dirt.
I begin with the cloud on its back,

the train at the horizon small & black
as a swarm of gnats,

with my right thumb
dumb as a puppy & squat & fat

as an old woman stooping over
the mess I have made of her garden;

& now the train is gnawing
its way through the meadow, going

like Columbus toward the end of the world.
The garden has dried to a dish of mud.

The tree's shadow is coming toward me
stiffly & slowly as an old woman's leg

in a black stocking
& now the clouds come carrying

their own white hankies, waving
good-bye & one bad child is squalling.

Seizure

This was the winter mother told time by my heart
ticking like a frayed fan belt in my chest.
This was the fifties & we were living on nothing
& what of her, the black girl, my own black nurse,
what of her who arrived on Greyhound in the heart
of so dramatic a storm it froze the sleeves at her wrists
& each nostril was rimed with white like salt on a glass,
what of her who came up the dark stair on the limp of her
own bad ticker, weary, arrogant, thin, her suitcase noosed
with rope, in the grip of a rage she came, a black woman,
into our white lives, like a splinter, & stayed. Charming
& brilliantly condescending, she leaned down to kiss "the baby,"
& hissed *my little princess* & hushed the Jordan & set the chariots
on the golden streets & *Mother*, I cried to her, & went out like a light.

Frying Trout While Drunk

Mother is drinking to forget a man
Who could fill the woods with invitations:
Come with me he whispered and she went
In his Nash Rambler, its dash
Where her knees turned green
In the radium dials of the '50s.
When I drink it is always 1953,
Bacon wilting in the pan on Cook Street
And mother, wrist deep in red water,
Laying a trail from the sink
To a glass of gin and back.
She is a beautiful, unlucky woman
In love with a man of lechery so solid
You could build a table on it
And when you did the blues would come to visit.
I remember all of us awkwardly at dinner,
The dark slung across the porch
And then mother's dress falling to the floor,
Buttons ticking like seeds spit on a plate.
When I drink I am too much like her—
The knife in one hand and in the other
The trout with a belly white as my wrist.
I have loved you all my life
She told him and it was true
In the same way that all her life
She drank, dedicated to the act itself,
She stood at this stove
And with the care of the very drunk
Handed him the plate.

. . .

Into the clearing of . . .
she climbed and stood

up from the black boots of her blackouts
into her body.

The coat wept upon her shoulder,
it hung upon her, a carcass heavy on a hook,

and in the sockets of the buttonholes
the buttons lolled and looked.

As she climbed into that clearing
it shook as it took her.

A fever wrote the sentence
and screwed it tight with ache

and the long hair of the grass grew silvery and weak,
lay greasily against the skull of dirt.

My mother was a figure armed with . . .
and came toward me

flew to me as though I were a sentence
that must be mended, that must be broken,

then ended, ended, ended.

She Is Six

She sleeps on a cot in the living room.
This is her father's mother's house.
And in the kitchen the men run their knife blades
Across the oilcloth with roses on the table
And grandmother cooks them steak and eggs.
She is pretending to be asleep but she is listening
To the men talking about their friends
And grandmother in her white dress
Walks back and forth past the door
And a hand reaches for salt and water.
Her father talks about divorce.
Now it is quiet.
Grandmother has left, her tight stockings
Showed rainbows,
And someone's upstairs undressing,
His dog tags making faint noise.
Her father walks into the room.
He is naked and there are certain
Parts of him that are shadows.
And he pulls the blankets to the floor
And then the sheet—as if not to wake her—
And he lifts her up and whispers his wife's name—
Rachel, Rachel
And he takes her hand, small with its clean nails,
And he puts it to the dark:
Oh Rae, Oh Rachel he says
And over his shoulder she can see
The long hall mirror framed in black wood
And she smells lavender in her father's hair
And then he gets up, first onto his hands
And knees like someone playing horse,
And puts her on the chair
And she sits and rocks like a deaf woman.

When Father Decided He Did Not Love Her Anymore

Tonight I will remember the model
With the wide, sad mouth
Who used to pose for father
Because I love the dangers of memory,
The boarded window and door,
Rooms where one bare bulb
Makes shadows swell up the wall.
And yet I recall only vaguely
The way her hem rustled on the floor
Like sand against tin
Laisse-moi tranquille, epicier,
It said because I want it to
Say something memorable.
I want her back
That brilliant farfetched woman
Who drank coffee in our garden
And the days father fed me
Absinthe through a sugar cube
So I would be asleep by noon
And wake to find Ramona posing
Naked with a tambourine.
Tonight the whole world is a garden
In which the immortal whispers
Something about art
And its opportunities:
Memory like a bolt of silk
In a tailor's arms
Can be made into anything
Especially misfortune,
Especially the year Ramona spent
In a wrath almost biblical
And so far from the world
Not even the moon could find
Her study in Paris
Where the doors opened to the river.

Outside Room Six

Down on my knees again, on the linoleum outside room six,
I polish it with the remnant of Grandpa's union suit,
and once again dead Grandma Fry looks down on me
from Paradise and tells me from the balcony of wrath
I am girlhood's one bad line of credit.

Every older girl I know is learning how to in a car,
while here I am, eye at the keyhole, watching Raoul,
who heats my dreams with his red hair, lights up my life
with his polished brogues, groans *Jesus, Jesus.*
I am little and stare into the dark until the whole small

town of lust emerges. I stare with envy, I stare and stare.
Now they are having cocktails. The drinks are dim lagoons
beneath their paper parasols. The air is stung with orange,
with lemon, a dash of Clorox, a dash of bitters;
black square, white square goes the linoleum.

Self-Portrait as Items in a Snowy Lithograph

I am the fox both sly and cowed
Wearing my delicate awkward legs through the forest

Leaving the breadcrumbs of my footprints on the blank page.
That is one self. The other is the black strikes of the trees—

A small gray hollow at the base of each
As though the snow had melted from their heat.

That isn't it.
The trees are the trees.

What then? The arrow in the bow?
What preys on fox?

Nothing but the mouth of the trap buried beneath its next step.
I am also that. And the snow that covers it.

Ordinary Objects

"Hic et ubique?"
—Hamlet to the Ghost

I am letting them stand
For everything I love.

The light's unsteady scale
Across the glass, the hard

Brown grit of ants among the roses,
The bittersweet

Everywhere I look I will see
Italy. The flowers will be full

Of prisons and churches,
Of women in black dresses, full

Of motorcycles and genuflecting.
The nightshade's dark, crooked stem

Is your street
And the water in the vase the sea's

Horizon tilting with the tilt
Of your ship. I am going to let

The daffodil be your mistress.
She is tired of you and stands

Looking at her feet.
In the fan's slow wind

The curtains reach for you.
I am full of grief. I am going

To lie down and die and be reborn
To come back as these roses

And wind myself thorn by
Thorn around your house

To fit into the nutshell
And the flat seed, the scar,

The door, the road, the web,
The moon's bald envious eye

Staring at you through the drapes.

Big Black Car

. . . anything with wheels
is a hearse in the making.
—Richard Miller

I thought, You'll never get me
anywhere near that motor's flattened
skull, the hoses' damp guts, the oil
pan with its tubes and fluids; I thought,
I'll never ride the black bargello
of the treads or be locked up
behind its locks and keys,
or stare at the empty sockets
of those headlights, the chrome
grill so glazed with light it blurs—oily, edible, about to melt.
You'll never get me into that back seat,
the ruptured upholstery hemorrhaging
batting is not for me, nor the spooky
odometer, nor the gas-gauge letters
spilled behind the cracked,
milky glass. The horn, like Saturn,
is suspended in its ring of steering wheel;
and below it the black tongue of the gas pedal,
the bulge of the brake, the stalk
of the stick shift, and I thought, You'll never . . .
But here I am, and there in the window
the tight black street comes unzipped
and opens to the snowy underthings,
the little white stitches and thorns
of a starry sky, and there, beyond
the world's open gate, eternity
hits me like a heart attack.

The Garden

Let us coax the stillness from the page   and let every leaf stand nakedly
in its own body   as though someone drew this place
let there be a garden   remote   perfect   and let him
visit upon the shoulders of its hills   the arrival
of the sun the moon   he has made everything that is marvelous
the bare limbs of every tree braceleted in green   the wrist of every river
braceleted by bridges   let this stillness be perfect and let us be still
to please him   he drew us here
hovering in the doorway of this scene   a small town hushed as a garden
where the crickets tumble through a round of song   then sleep
let us sleep with them it is night for a long time   sweet with darkness
because he loved sweetness   and quiet   loved the perfect
man   the perfect woman   let us be pleasing to him   who has given us
the excellent clothing of ourselves   when there was nothing
let us try for him   to be nothing
as we stand in the doorway of the story   in the towns
in the new world   let us try
to withhold ourselves from the story of ourselves
as he would have wanted   the man   the woman
hovering at the threshold   just at the beginning   of the story.

The Technology of Love

I loved the women of Ely, Nevada, who drank, wept,
and waited out their pasts among the lint
and pins of Roman Catholic self-denial.
Tonight I have come home to watch the girls
of those girls climb the steps of Saint Agnes
while I sit studying the forest of their lit candles
in the open door until the Erie comes past,
black as a seizure, right on schedule.
As a child I sweated out the evening watching
the windows burn in the house of prostitution
that opened when the whole town slept—
even the tiers of saucers at the Beaufort Cafeteria,
even the blues in Ruby's black Victrola.
No matter what I remember I remember that
when she walked down the street all the men
grew still as flags on a still day; I remember
my Great Aunt Ada telling her I told you so
about the sailor whose shadow did a rumba
on Ruby's wall and left her in a flat blaze
of remorse where she drifted for years
visiting every island in the long archipelago of lust.
I loved helping her home, dead drunk,
through the streets of Ely; this world
is no earthly paradiso she told my grandfather
who being my grandfather was looking at the madam
in her black capris, or studying the technology of love:
pawnshop windows filled with wedding rings and guns,
that summer when, glum and drunk, Ruby drove
her blue Impala into the cottonwood on Lagunitas Boulevard.
The only thing that bored Ruby more than God was poetry,
so tonight I have come home to write something plain
as a woman in her grave and watch the girls come out of church
counting up their sins and graces, safe in this last outpost
of the conventional unlike Ruby who is a remembrance and dread

that go beyond what I can bear remembering and further, so deep
she sweeps away all doctrines and boast, that woman teasing
her lures against the current, that ark in its loose gown of oared water.

Heartsick

I had enough bad luck that summer,
I had enough bad weather, too, the sun
lacquered the windows across the street
that were shut against the heat of noon;
staring out at them from behind the dim
screen of the terminal I knew my neighbors
were sweating in their dark bedrooms,
foreheads leaked on by cooling compresses.

I was spending the summer getting diagnosed,
trudging the hot and littered streets for weekly
visits to a doctor so expensive and remote
my voice shook when I called for my
appointment, and even now he seems
to me a tall white blur in a white coat.
I was not myself. In that heat
my heart had reestablished its old
bad habit of skipping a beat so that
suddenly I felt like a factory out of work,
all the machinery went still, the silence
was deafening and quick, dying seemed
within, then out of reach.

I throve on this medical melodrama, my ill health
sustained me over the bad places until
the police called at seven A.M. to tell me
Raoul Fiori had been picked up for vagrancy
on a traffic island in Lake Street and, not awake,
I said, I'm sorry I don't know any Raoul.
Then there was a blank place, the sound of a precinct,
not sound, really, but to sound what a Xerox
is to print and then a voice—his—but so condensed,
tiny, light, like an insect, like the ghost of a ghost,
Lynn, I need a place to spend the night, it said.

I was not impressed. I did not want to be
disturbed by reveries or guilt, but, all right,
yes, I said, take a taxi, I'll pay
when you get here. And I did.
Because when the door of the taxi
opened and he ducked out into the sun,
sorrow and love kicked me so hard
in the chest my heart just stopped;
it seemed to say, I cannot bear it, you
go on without me. And I did, I walked
down the walk and stood while he
handed my money to the driver
and everything began to take on preternatural

detail. I noticed the shoulder of his leather jacket
scratched and scuffed, and my heart rose up
out of its stutter, its limp, when the next beat
seemed to drip from it achingly, infinitely
slowly, and never arrive, and that dark barn
behind the Blue Lite opened its doors to me
again and I let myself be backed against
the dirty bale, warm against my butt, as this boy,
part gall, part oil, ran his hand below my boned bra
and whispered, *Is this the Maginot Line?*
while I grew just idiotic with anxiety and lust.

Blonde Bombshell

Love is boring and passé, all that old baggage,
the bloody bric-a-brac, the bad, the gothic,
retrograde, obscurantist hum and drum of it
needs to be swept away. So, night after night,
we sit in the dark of the Roxy beside grandmothers
with their shanks tied up in the tourniquets
of rolled stockings and open ourselves, like earth
to rain, to the blue fire of the movie screen
where love surrenders suddenly to gangsters
and their cuties. There in the narrow,
mote-filled finger of light, is a blonde,
so blonde, so blinding, she is a blizzard, a huge
spook, and lights up like the sun the audience
in its galoshes. She bulges like a deuce coupe.
When we see her we say good-bye to Kansas.
She is everything spare, cool, and clean,
like a gas station on a dark night and the cold
dependable light of rage coming in on schedule like a bus.

The White Dress

What does it feel like to be this shroud
on a hanger, this storm cloud hanging
in the closet? We itch to feel it, it itches
to be felt, it feels like an itch—

encrusted with beading, it's an eczema
of sequins, rough, gullied, riven,
puckered with stitchery, a frosted window
against which we long to put our tongues,

a vase for holding the long-stemmed
bouquet of a woman's body.
Or it's armor and it fits like a glove.
The buttons run like rivets down the front.

When we're in it we're machinery,
a cutter nosing the ocean of a town.
Right now it's lonely locked up
in the closet; while we're busy

fussing at our vanity, it hangs there
in the drooping waterfall of itself,
a road with no one on it, bathed
in moonlight, rehearsing its lines.

Self-Portrait at Eighteen

Today I became my own secret admirer, unearthing
from the junk—the boxes of napkins tatted by Grandmother
and Great Aunt Tiny, the cobwebby bulk of table linens
that covered the scab of scratched deal that was their kitchen
table where they gave thanks and passed the faded confetti
of the succotash—this photograph. It is not a flash of family
dinner, but a luminous window, the faded wash of clouds
strung up in Talamone. Somewhere at the rim a somewhat darker,
rumpled mass of—what?—the photographer's jacket, or the blanket
where, after buying two tabs of acid from a boy who sold
a handful along the shore, we made love and then set out to
sabotage respectability or, at least in my case, self-regard.
In the foreground a fringe of reeds suggests the landscape
blinked at this girl-stretched-naked-on-the-sand,
although *stretched* implies passivity, loss of will, and clearly
this is a willful, though awkward, abandonment, an act
of exposure not merely meant but mutinous. Uncanny
the resemblance of the pose—awkward, although not innocent—
to an inexperienced lounge singer, maybe a girl leaning
uneasily against a black piano; she has knuckled under
to convention but clearly not enough or generously.
Still I love the delicate bones of my pelvis (the bony repose
that suggests, as well, the sculptures on sarcophagi)
in this photograph which a not-quite-forgotten-enough
photographer entitled: *Portrait of a Woman, Nude.*

Portrait of the Author

Today I write about the house
of the body and about myself,

its shadowy proprietor,
coming and going.

Above the street, beside a fan
and a half inch of bourbon

floating in a tumbler, someone's
white face pokes a hole

in a dark window. It's me,
in the body of a man named Raoul.

The rain stings the window
and the nothing beyond.

The rain throbs steadily
as the heart's dull return and lob.

Bending over the woman on the bed,
Raoul says, *Take off your dress.*

I'll take my dress off, the woman says.
And then the sibilant whisper

of a black silk frock.
(*A what?*)

Frock. On the floor.
Also hosiery. Also black.

Suddenly naked or wearing
only flawless technique

and the dark eyes of staring
breasts, the story ends

either (A)

Bending over her
beautiful and tragic face

against the pillows, Raoul says,
Oh Lynn, Lynn, you bring me to my knees.

Or (B)

Gazing up into my own
beautiful and tragic face, I say,

Oh, Raoul, you bring me to my knees.

The Politics of Narrative: Why I Am a Poet

Jill's a good kid who's had some tough luck. But that's another story. It's a day when the smell of fish from Tib's hash house is so strong you could build a garage on it. We are sitting in Izzy's where Carl has just built us a couple of solid highballs. He's okay, Carl is, if you don't count his Roamin' Hands and Rushin' Fingers. Then again, that should be the only trouble we have in this life. Anyway, Jill says, "Why don't you tell about it? Nobody ever gets the poet's point of view." I don't know, maybe she's right. Jill's just a kid, but she's been around; she knows what's what.

So, I tell Jill, we are at Izzy's just like now when he comes in. And the first thing I notice is his hair, which has been Vitalis-ed into submission. But it won't work, and it gives him a kind of rumpled-your-boudoir-or-mine look. I don't know why I noticed that before I noticed his face. Maybe it was just the highballs doing the looking. Anyway, then I see his face, and I'm telling you—I'm telling Jill—this is a masterpiece of a face.

But—and this is the god's own truth—I'm tired of beauty. Really. I know, given all that happened, this must sound kind of funny, but it made me tired just to look at him. That's how beautiful he was, and how much he spelled T-R-O-U-B-L-E. So I threw him back. I mean, I didn't say it, I say to Jill, with my mouth. But I said it with my eyes and my shoulders. I said it with my heart. I said, Honey, I'm throwing you back. And looking back, that was the worst, I mean the worst thing—bar none—that I could have done, because it drew him like horseshit draws flies. I mean, he didn't walk over and say, "Hello, girls; hey, you with the dark hair, your indifference draws me like horseshit draws flies."

But he said it with his eyes. And then he smiled. And that smile was a gas station on a dark night. And as wearying as all the rest of it. I am many things, but dumb isn't one of them. And here is where I say to Jill, "I just can't go on." I mean, how we get from the smile into the bedroom, how it all happens, and what all happens, just bores me. I am a conceptual storyteller. In fact, I'm a conceptual liver. I prefer the cookbook to the actual meal. Feeling bores me. That's why I write poetry. In poetry you just give the instructions to the reader and say, "Reader, you go on from here." And what I like about poetry is its readers, because those are giving people. I mean, those are people you can trust to get the job done. They pull their own weight. If I had to have someone at my back in a dark alley, I'd want it to be a poetry reader. They're not like some people, who maybe do it right if you tell them, "Put this foot down, and now put that one in front of the other, button your coat, wipe your nose."

So, really, I do it for the readers who work hard and, I feel, deserve something better than they're used to getting. I do it for the working stiff. And I write for people, like myself, who are just tired of the trickle-down theory where somebody spends pages and pages on some fat book where everything including the draperies, which happen to be *burnt orange*, are described, and, further, are some *metaphor* for something. And this whole boggy waste trickles down to the reader in the form of a little burp of feeling. God, I hate prose. I think the average reader likes ideas.

"A sentence, unlike a line, is not a station of the cross." I said this to the poet Mark Strand. I said, "I could not stand to write prose; I could not stand to have to write things like 'the draperies were burnt orange and the carpet was brown.'" And he said, "You could do it if that's all you did, if that was the beginning and end of your novel." So please, don't ask me for a little trail of bread crumbs to get from the smile to the bedroom to the death at the end, although you can ask me a lot about death. That's all I like, the very beginning and the very end. I haven't got the stomach for the rest of it.

I don't think many people do. But, like me, they're either too afraid or too polite to say so. That's why the movies are such a disaster. Now *there's* a form of popular culture that doesn't have a clue. Movies should be five minutes long. You should go in, see a couple of shots, maybe a room with orange draperies and a rug. A voice-over would say, "I'm having a hard time getting Raoul from the hotel room into the elevator." And bang, that's the end. The lights come on, everybody walks out full of sympathy because this is a shared experience. Everybody in that theater knows how hard it is to get Raoul from the hotel room into the elevator. Everyone has had to do boring, dogged work. Everyone has lived a life that seems to inflict upon every vivid moment the smears fingerings, and pawings of plot and feeling. Everyone has lived under this oppression. In other words, everyone has had to eat shit—day after day, the endless meals they didn't want, those dark, half-gelatinous lakes of gravy that lay on the plate like an ugly rug and that wrinkled clump of reddish-orange roast beef that looks like it was dropped onto your plate from a great height. God what a horror: getting Raoul into the elevator.

And that's why I write poetry. In poetry, you don't do that kind of work.

Self-Portrait

Tiresome, tiresome is the poet
Recumbent on the davenport
Lost in raptures of self-regard.
Give me poetry, but pure
Before *charcuterie* and *bistro*
And distracted poses in tilted mirrors.
I am what is wrong with America.
Standing debauched, bereft,
Empty-handed for first one
Eternal verity and then another,
I am tired of all my yawn and barter.
How boring beauty is:
All chives and savannas,
The lush populations of grasses,
Are one vast atelier for the abstract.
Despite my lovely diction
I am going to die
Lying on an iron bed in stocking feet.
Oh no, oh no says the portrait
But so beautifully it is almost yes.

Dressing the Parts

Here I comes.
—Anne Lauterbach

So, here we are,
I am a kind of diction

I can walk around in
clothed in the six-inch heels

of *arrogation* and *scurrility.*
And what are you

wearing? Is it those boxer
things again? I hope it is

those boxer things
and nothing else

except your eyes;
I like your eyes; do you

like the way my feet
are long, narrow,

with toenails like tiny television screens?
And hair is important.

A fog of hair floating
above the fields of the body.

Or the body as bald
as a truffle,

very French—
swine on leashes.

Like you, my pig.
I'm your truffle and

for you
reading is eating.

Is too.

When you were at the Brasserie
eating—

crêpes fourrées, and
légumes à la Grecque, and

and, and—
you felt like you had read all of

Leaves of Grass at one sitting.
Wait, I see something

between your teeth:
it is a kiss as wet

and mobile as a gourami
in an aquarium.

Oh. God. Yes.
Describe the lips.

Describe what
the lips are wearing.

Is it that color called
Red-as-the-roofs-of-Brest?

That color that the lips
of the you are wearing?

That *you*, reader,
That you are wearing.

Starlet in Satin Dressing Gown

First of all—a road with no one on it,
almost Asian, the misty wash of shadow and light
which, nevertheless, we must not forget
is the road to hell. So, she is not a woman, really,
but a felony in a bathrobe; (even the pale, linty,
fluff of her hairdo is a fuse aching to be lit)—
a woman like a hand grenade.

The cord around her waist suggests
the ecclesiastical: Our Lady of Burned Bridges,
murmurs every mother in the audience's every head.
We know her, she is everything we've been
warned against. She has a big X through her
and the rules are strict: says the severe cut,
look but don't touch. Don't even look.

Homage to Sharon Stone

It's early morning. This is the "before,"
the world hanging around in its wrapper,
blowsy, frumpy, doing nothing: my
neighbors, hitching themselves to the roles
of the unhappily married, trundle their three
mastiffs down the street. I am writing this
book of poems. My name is Lynn Emanuel.
I am wearing a bathrobe and curlers; from
my lips, a Marlboro drips ash on the text.
It is the third of September 20**.
And as I am writing this in my trifocals
and slippers, across the street, Sharon Stone,
her head swollen with curlers, her mouth
red and narrow as a dancing slipper,
is rushed into a black limo. And because
these limos snake up and down my street,
this book will be full of sleek cars nosing
through the shadowy ocean of these words,
giving to the street,
(Liberty Avenue in Pittsburgh, PA),
and to the book I am writing, an aspect
that is both glamorous and funereal.
My name is Lynn Emanuel, and in this
book I play the part of someone writing
a book, and I take the role seriously,
just as Sharon Stone takes seriously
the role of the diva. I watch the dark
cars disappear her and in my poem
another Lexus erupts like a big animal
at the cool trough of a shady curb. So,
when you see this black car, do not think
it is a Symbol For Something. It is just
Sharon Stone driving past the house
of Lynn Emanuel who is, at the time,
trying to write a book of poems.

Or you could think of the black car as
Lynn Emanuel, because, really, as an author,
I have always wanted to be a car, even
though most of the time I have to be
the "I," or the woman hanging wash;
I am a woman, one minute, then I am a man,
I am a carnival of Lynn Emanuels:
Lynn in the red dress; Lynn sulking
behind the big nose of my erection;
then I am the train pulling into the station
when what I would really love to be is
Gertrude Stein spying on Sharon Stone
at six in the morning. But enough about
that, back to the interior decorating:
On the page, the town looks bald
and dim so I turn up the amps on
the radioactive glances of bad boys.
In a kitchen, I stack pans sleek with
grease, and on a counter there is a roast
beef red as a face in a tantrum. Amid all
this bland strangeness is Sharon Stone,
who, like an engraved invitation, is asking
me, *Won't you, too, play a role*? I do not
choose the black limo rolling down the street
with the golden stare of my limo headlights
bringing with me the sun, the moon, and
Sharon Stone. It is nearly dawn; the sun
is a fox chewing her foot from the trap;
every bite is a wound and every wound
is a red window, a red door, a red road.
My name is Lynn Emanuel. I am the writer
trying to unwrite the world that is all around her.

On Waking after Dreaming of Raoul

If Freud was right and dreams of falling are
dreams of having fallen then you must have been
the beautiful declivity of that hill, Raoul,
the speed was so seductive and the brakes so
unreliable, and so intricate and so abstract
that when I touched them they squeaked like a jar lid
coming loose and I was embarrassed, but not sad,
at being the one flat wheel that bumped down the hill
in an unsteady gulp of denial—oh no oh no oh no—
until I woke up chilly, damp, my breath unsteady.

In order to recover I sit at the desk studying the Order
of the Holy Ghost Retreat and Old Age Home
until dusk comes down the street elm by elm, here
where they've managed to cure them with a tincture
so poisonous the leaves, though living, are frail
and blanched. I think of you, Ruby Fiori's
half-brother, a thief, and a cook.
Because what good is it anymore, pretending
I didn't love you; after all these years you must
be jailed or dead, and it is a relief to give up
reticence which as you once said is merely
impetuosity held tightly in check.

Over the gold swells of sunset lawns the old
men come rolling in their iron chairs, pushed
around by nuns, their open mouths are *Os*
of permanent dismay. Far away the stars are
a fine talcum dusting my mother's one good black
dress, those nights she gunned the DeSoto
around Aunt Ada's bed of asters while you shortened
the laces of my breath. Despite the nuns, despite
my mother and my own notions of how bad girls
end up educated and alone, the door opens and you

walk in, naked, you, narrow and white
as the fishing knife's pearl handle, and you kiss me
until my resolve grows as empty as the dress
from which I step, both brave and willful.
I loved you, although I didn't know it yet,
anymore than these old men on the dole
of some nun's affectionate disdain
knew that they would end up poor,
mortgaged to a ghost, and living in a place like this.

Inspiration

I am tired of the tundra of the mind,
where a few shabby thoughts hunker
around a shabby fire. All day from my window
I watch girls and boys hanging out
in the dark arcades of adolescent desire.

Tonight, everything is strict with cold,
the houses closed, the ice botched by skaters.
I am tired of saying things about the world,
and yet, sometimes, these streets are so
slick and bold they remind me of the wet

zinc bar at the Café Marseilles, and suddenly the sea
is green and lust is everywhere in a red cravat,
leaning on his walking stick and whispering,
I am a city, you are my pilgrim,
meet me this evening. Love, Pierre.

And so I have to get up and walk downstairs
just to make sure the city's still secure
in its leafless and wintery slime
and it still is and yet somewhere on that
limitless, starlit seacoast of my past,

Pierre's red tie burns like a small fire.
And all at once my heart stumbles like a
drunken sailor, and I am adrift in the *bel aujourd'hui* of Pittsburgh.

Spite—Homage to Sylvia Plath

I stamped my foot and shook my fist and wept,
I wanted to be one of that glamorous sorority of the dead,
to feel the rib cage opened, the knocking of the heart let out,
I wanted to lie with the paperweight of the Bible on my chest;
I wanted the return, the rebirth, to be the root you fell over,
the curb of earth that made you stumble. I wanted to be the little
poisonous selves that grew up in your gardens, the henbane,
and belladonna, the lovely, misnamed hens-and-chickens;
I wanted revenge, to be the meek inheriting, beyond hurt and worry,
I wanted to come back as the vegetal, the spectacular amphibian welter
of the swamp, the pond, the marsh, the fen, to begin again and again,
I wanted to be no mind, all flesh, no thinking, all feeling, just *IS*
taking everything into its bog, its tar pit, into the locked box of unbeing.

Walt, I Salute You!

From the Year of Our Lord 20**,
from the Continent of the Amnesias,
from the back streets of Pittsburgh
from the little lit window in the attic
of my mind where I sit brooding and smoking
like a hot iron, Walt, I salute you!

Here we are. In Love! In a Poem!
Slouching toward rebirth in our hats and curls!
Walt, I'm just a woman, chaperoned, actual, vague, and hysterical.
Outwardly, my life is one of irreproachable tedium;
inside, like you, I am in my hydroelectric mode.
The infinite and abstract current of my description
launches itself at the weakling grass. Walt, everything I see I am!
Nothing is too small for my interest in it.
I am undone in the multiplication
of my perceptions. Mine is a life alive
with the radioactivity of other lives.

I am every dog and hairpin. They are me! I am you!
All is connected in the great seethe of seeing and being,
the great oceans and beaches of speeding and knowing.

Walt! You have me by the throat!
Everywhere I turn you rise up insurmountable and near.

You have already been every Conestoga headed to California
that broke down in a cul-de-sac of cannibalism in the Rockies.
You have been every sprouting metropolis rerouted
through three generations of industrialists.
You, the sweat of their workers' brows! You, their hatred of poets!

You have been women! Women with white legs, women with black mustaches,
waitresses with their hands glued to their rags on the counter,
waitresses in Dacron who light up the room with their serious wattage.
Yes! You are magically filling up, like milk in a glass, the white
nylon uniform, the blocky shoes with their slab of rubber sole!
Your hair is a platinum helmet, a name plate pinned above your breast.

And you have been places! You have been junkyards with their rusted Hoovers,
the pistils of wilted umbrellas.
And then, on the horizon (you have been the horizon!)
Walt, you are a whole small town erupting!
The streets black and slick as iron skillets.
The tawdry buildings. The rooms rented.
And now, in total hallucination and inhabitation, tired of being yourself—
Walt, the champ, the chump, the cheeky—you become me!
My every dark and slanderous thought. Walt, I salute you!
And therefore myself! In our enormous hats! In our huge mustaches!
We can't hide! We recognize ourselves!

The Occupation

I used to love reading the great poets and the words that hovered like bees at the lines' cut edges scythed by their commas. But tonight, beyond my locked door, the ground takes charge of caving in. Somewhere, the windows in kitchens smolder and soldier onward toward a glass of gin. I long for its coffin, the heat of its sleep. Dear Sleep, help me sheet the furniture in the rooms of the brain. I will not look underneath at the black ache of the table or wake the furnishings into breathing. I will cut open the vein that feeds the beat of the pendulum. I once read the great poets until my heart was blown open. Now, whenever I stoop over the hard desk of my heart—the soldiers come. Troy is burned.

. . .

Hello, Mallarmé,

And adieu, Walt Whitman.

Whitman, I fell in love with capitalism
because of your commas

in lines that cannot decide
if they are crowbars for rending and tearing or sutures for holding the wound together.

Your nouns are many and alive.
But tonight my tongue is silent,

asleep and . . .

. . .

Born by the sagging branch, the crawl of snow beyond the sash—

Page, I am so weary of your black-and-white.
The whole street becomes an illustration of you.

Why do the trees have too many
syllables or too few?

Outside my room it is 4 A.M. Dear Mallarmé, it's me again.

. . .

When asked if he would not name it—

Mallarmé looked at the sail of his little boat
about to sail the Seine and said,
This is one page that will not be written on.

I too have launched a craft as frail as—

But now

I annul the jib and mizzen and masts,
the harp of town and shore.

America, you don't need poetry.
Could we not go back to the way things were:

a page that once lay as bare as moon
above the black lapping of leaves?

Before you were a link in my chain, before I was money for your tolls?

Before you and I were forced to speak?

In English in a Poem

I am giving a lecture on poetry
to the painters who creak like saddles
in their black leather jackets in the studio,
where a fire is burning like a painting of
a fire; I am explaining my current work
on the erotics of narrative. It is night.
Overhead the moon's naked heel dents
the sky, the crickets ignite themselves
into a snore, and the painters yawn
lavishly waiting for me to say Something
About Painting, the way your dog, when
you are talking, listens for the words Good Dog.

"Your indifference draws me like horses draw flies,"
I say while noticing in the window the peonies
throbbing with pulses, the cindery crows seething
over the lawn. "Nevertheless," I continue, "I call
your attention to the fact that, in this poem, what was
once just a pronoun is now a pronoun talking about
a peony while you sit in a room somewhere unmoved
by this. And that's okay. Gertrude Stein said America
was a *space filled with moving,* but I hate being moving.
If you want to *feel* go to the movies, because poetry
has no intention of being moving; it is perhaps one
of the few things left in America that is not moving.

And yet, I am a fatalist when it comes to art
in English, because in English
even a simile is a story and there is no trip
so predictable that some poem won't take it."
And just as I am finishing my lecture, here
is the snowy hem of the end of the page
and one of the painters says to me, "Actually,
I found that very moving. Get in the car.
I'll drive you home."

A Poem Like an Automobile Can Take You Anywhere,

but you have to wait until Mother gets loaded
on the Greyhound and the bus blotted up
by the black of tobacco at the end of Rook Street
in Bannock, Georgia; until someone's
Aunt Rita, up to her neck again in hot water,
dries the last damp dimple and sweeps away
the constellation of Dier Kiss spilled on her

dressing table, before the plot can come lunging,
purring up to the door of the rental cottage.
It says: We'll go for a spin, and you say, *D'accord*!
thinking of Paris where a vague and soigné sun
rises forever above the seriously drunk, thinking
of Greece where you can fall in love with the sailors.

And suddenly the room's perfumed with lust
the sheet's a slick and dangerous road
where coupes of French hoods fishtail
like downed power lines and lurch and zoom
and billboards—Giant! White! Immaculate!—
are flying past and the boglands are in bloom.

And your curiosity begins to travel
like a caravan, each pack animal loaded
with its weight of questions. Why has
the Gare de Lyon bulging at the horizon
huge, many, tough, turned out to be
a grandpa in his waders among the sycamores?

There in the dark oblong of the windshield
a field of wheat comes swarming toward you
and hicks with open arms welcome you
to Ely, its parlors filled with the little iambs
of Granny's rocker, its sky damp and gray and chilly.

Lost in this wilderness, American and corny,
you stare at the trees and compose new
stanzas of such extravagant uncertainty that,
like "Uncle Raoul" whom you watched on
your knees through the keyhole, who lit up
your life with his burnished lassoes, they groan,
Jesus, Jesus, enough, enough.

The Past

Where did she come from, that dig
in the ribs? Who is she to pretend
she's me and to take on that ditched-in,
hopeless tone? Who is this phony
yokel? This two-dollar bill, this
pig knuckle? Listen, I tell her,
my name is Lynn Collins Emanuel,
someone whose whole manner says
I'm over-educated but recovering,
I have been to Europe and I don't
even recall that stain in the road
that you refer to as Ely, Nevada;
oh please, I think, give me a break,
woman, I mean who would believe
this arms-akimbo-in-faded-calico
West Coast depiction of the West?
Get out of here with your fibs
and lesions, your deaf ear wired
to its hearing aid, your coughs
and wattles. I know stories about
Gertrude Stein in her silk socks
drunk on Bordeaux in the garden.
What do I want to sit at your table for,
to be passed the faded confetti
of the succotash, the turkey
trussed like a hostage? Listen,
I am money in the bank, swank,
with it, well informed, full
of a Semitic glamour, doleful,
sleek and dark, shit, honey,
how did you get by the bouncer,
editor-within-me, Mr. Right?
And why am I now, like a new tenant,
moving into the little varicosity

on your left calf, the nylons knotted
just above the knee and further
into the hands that held that soft
gray lump of rag and washed,
and washed again the greasy
Formica of the dinner table?
How did I get to be at the head
of a long line of unlucky
women with their propensity
for poverty, influenza,
weak chests, and bad judgment,
how did their troubles get to be mine?
And no, I don't know who
could be in that hand-dug grave
at the Rosebud Cemetery, the little
dusty picket fence of teeth smiling up
from that too-shallow niche is
not mine. I don't know who
she is. I've never seen her.
I was in Paris at the time.

inside gertrude stein

Right now as I am talking to you and as you are being talked to, without letup, it is becoming clear that gertrude stein has hijacked me and that this feeling that you are having now as you read this, that this is what it feels like to be inside gertrude stein. This is what it feels like to be a huge typewriter in a dress. Yes, I feel we have gotten inside gertrude stein, and of course it is dark inside the enormous gertrude, it is like being locked up in a refrigerator lit only by a smiling rind of cheese. Being inside gertrude is like being inside a monument made of a cloud which is always moving across the sky which is also always moving. Gertrude is a huge galleon of cloud anchored to the ground by one small tether, yes, I see it down there; do you see that tiny snail glued to the tackboard of the landscape? That is alice. So, I am inside gertrude; we belong to each other she and I, and it is so wonderful because I have always been a thin woman inside of whom a big woman is screaming to get out, and she's out now and if a river could type this is how it would sound, pure and complicated and enormous. Now we are lilting across the countryside, and we are talking, and if the wind could type it would sound like this, ongoing and repetitious, abstracting and stylizing everything, like our famous haircut painted by Picasso. Because when you are inside our haircut you understand that all the flotsam and jetsam of hairdo have been cleared away (like the forests from the New World) so that the skull can show through grinning and feasting on the alarm it has created. I am now, alarmingly, inside gertrude's head and I am thinking that I may only be a thought she has had when she imagined that she and alice were dead and gone and someone had to carry on the work of being gertrude stein, and so I am receiving, from beyond the grave, radioactive isotopes of her genius saying, take up my work, become gertrude stein.

Because someone must be gertrude stein, someone must save us from the literalists and realists, and narratives of the beginning and end, someone must be a river that can type. And why not I? Gertrude is insisting on the fact that while I am a subgenius, weighing one hundred five pounds, and living in a small town with an enormous furry male husband who is always in his Cadillac Eldorado driving off to sell something to people who do not deserve the bad luck of this merchandise in their lives—that these facts would not be a problem for gertrude stein. Gertrude and I feel that, for instance, in *Patriarchal Poetry* when (like an avalanche that can type) she is burying the patriarchy, still there persists a sense of condescending affection. So, while I'm a thin, heterosexual subgenious, nevertheless gertrude has chosen me as her tool, just as she chose the patriarchy as her tool for ending the patriarchy. And because I have become her tool, now, in a sense, gertrude is inside me. It's tough. Having gertrude inside me is like having swallowed an ocean liner that can type, and while I feel like a very small coat closet with a bear in it, gertrude and I feel that I must tell you that gertrude does not care. She is using me to get her message across, to say, I am lost, I am beset by literalists and narratives of the beginning and middle and end, help me. And so, yes, I say, yes, I am here, gertrude, because we feel, gertrude and I, that there is a real urgency in our voice (like a sob that can type) and that things are very bad for her because she is lost, beset by the literalists and realists, her own enormousness crushing her, and we must find her and take her into ourselves, even though I am the least likely of saviors and have been chosen perhaps as a last resort, yes, definitely, gertrude is saying to me, you are the least likely of saviors, you are my last choice and my last resort.

IV

My Life

Like Jonas by the fish was I received by it,
swung and swept in its dark waters,
driven to the deeps by it and beyond many rocks.
Without any touching of its teeth, I tumbled into it
with no more struggle than a mote of dust
entering the door of a cathedral, so muckle were its jaws.
How heel over head was I hurled down
the broad road of its throat, stopped inside
its chest wide as a hall, and like Jonas I stood up
asking where the beast was and finding it nowhere,
there in grease and sorrow I build my bower.

Kiss

In the cooking pot my aunt's long spoon pets the lamb's
Severed head, anoints with oil its one terrible eye
Until it weeps at the flowers on her dress.
Where there was body once, now there is iron and fire.
I am here to help. I am here to put my hand under
The lamb's chin and tip it back as though for a kiss.
I am here to help the lamb with the axe
That halves the skull as I have heard my aunt halve
Her husband's name at night. I/saac.
The body cannot die. In the hard push of meadow
Behind the empty house I have seen the lamb's body
Ride a spit of peeled plum under my uncle's hand.
I have seen the lamb lie down in the fire and rise
To its cleft hooves. Through the dark archway
Of the cut neck I have watched the heart leak
Fire and flower a dry foam of ash.
The body cannot die. I can see this.
When the throat is tilted to let the smoke loose
The lamb's shadow crawls forward, licks, then swallows
The whole rough tongue of stones where I lie.
It is too quiet. I can feel the uneven knocking
Of my heart like someone tired hobbling across a yard.
Death is nothing.
It is fire looking for a place to start. It is a word
On the tip of the lamb's halved tongue, a kiss,
The smoke carrying the green wood into the firmament.

Grieving Was

not the summer of aspic
and cold veal. It was so hot

the car seat stung my thighs
and the rearview mirror swam

with mirage. In the back seat
the leather grip was noosed by twine.

We were not poor but we had
the troubles of the poor.

She who had been that soft snore
beside the Nytol, open-mouthed,

was gone, somewhere, somewhere
there was a bay, there was a boat,

there was a scold in mother's mouth.
What I remember best

is the way everything came and went
in the window of my brief attention.

At the wake I was beguiled
by the chromium yellow lemon pies.

The grandfather clock's pendant
of unaffordable gold told the quarter hour.

The hearse rolled forward over the *O*s
of its own surprise.

Dying Was

First I lay down
and then my senses began their climb
into the dark above me. Seeing, hearing
leapt away like goats I saw once in that hill
town in Tuscany, or like the day I stood and looked
on the Mediterranean's voluptuous and wrinkled bed,
now I gazed down on the immense miniature of this
landscape: the chimney of the throat stove in,
the collar of the larynx undone, even the knotted
grain of thumbprint was worn away. Good-bye thumb
and wrist, licked back by all the tiny hungers of ants
to the bare tree branches of the phalanges. Winter
had come and I was lunch, sumptuous, I who had been
a thin weed, a hank, was now a wide meadow, a marsh,
slick, fetid, damp, a swamp, I brewed and stank
until, mercifully, we came to the brain's convolvulus,
that wet coral, oceany and spacious, even that must be
lugged away like a big vegetable; I was an orphan,
and looked down now on the prairie, the waving
grass that licked up the last that I'd become,
but *I* looked down on them,
there was that *I*, a terrible cloud, a thinking wind.
That was the final terror, that I wept and could not die.

• • •

I tried to flatter myself into extinction, tried to bury alive in a landslide of disparagement ego and subjectivity and the first-person singular pronoun. I ran identity to ground with the dogs of irony; I tried to kill, bury, burn, embalm, and erase the outlines of me, mummify myself in the damp wrappings of surrealism, sever and rearrange me with Stein's cubisms, break, buy, bribe, drive a stake through me; tried to whip to death the whole frumpish horse-and-buggy, essentialist, runs-in-the-blood notion I had of who "I" was; like Stein I tried to bleed the bloody paragraph to death, killed the semicolon with the machete of my wit, tried to censor and edit, rewrite and emend me, my belief in lifeblood, marrow, core, and fiber; tried to swap my DNA at the DNA supermarket I read about in Philip K. Dick. So what is I still doing here? Why is I having to keep its eye peeled? Its eye on the ball? Trying to steer by some dim star, that small, raw planet of self-loathing hammered into the night ahead? Why is I hauled forth over this choppy terrain like a tug on the rough boulevards of a black river? And by whom?

. . .

While my mother lies in a hospital bed tethered to the earth
by the guy wires of two IVs, I run the streets
with the snare her skin throws over me,
the gristle of our skull more prominent, the hair draining from our head.
I run until sobs sough through the sieve of us.
I run, shutting first one of her eyes then the other: the left that gripped
handle by handle, the objects in their windows, the right that drunkenly
wobbled. Rooms close their shutters until the right lid drops
its curtain, smothers its sight, so now the left mothers me
among the shadows where we are so weary with the weight
of us our breath almost cannot, cannot, cannot, cannot,
nor our lips, nor our knees, and the hard darkness is padlocked with a huge
heart, no place to put a key or lock or unlock.

Ars Poetica

Personal experiences are chains and balls
fatally drawn to the magnetic personality.
I have always been a poet
who poured herself into the shrouds
of experience's tight dresses so that a reader could try to get a feel
for the real me, metaphorically speaking, of course.

I bore experience's leashes and tourniquets.
I stuffed myself deep into the nooses of its collars.
I was equipped. I was like a ship plated with the armor of experience,
nosing the seas which are its seas.

But now I have other things to do. I will not write about dying
my hair blonde-on-black for my post-post-feminist project. The wicked must be punished.
The innocent exalted, butchers called forth for the slaughter of the lambs, and doctors
called from their face-lifts to perform amputations.
I hear the call to rise out of the trance of myself
into the surcease of the dying world.

Since the war began I have discovered
(1) My Life Is Unimportant and (2) My Life Is Boring.
But now, as Gertrude Stein wrote from Culoz in 1943,
Now, we have an occupation.

Halfway Through the Book I'm Writing

This is the wonderful thing about art,
it can bring back the dead . . .

My father dies and is buried in his Brooks Brothers suit.
But I can't seem to keep him underground.
Suddenly, I turn around and there he is just
as I'm getting a handle on the train-pulls—
into-the-station poem. "What gives?"
I ask him. "I'm alone and dead," he says,
and I say, "Father, there's nothing I can do about
all that. Get your mind off it. Help me with the poem

about the train." "I hate the poem about the train,"
he says. But since he's dead and I'm a patient woman
I turn back to the poem in which the crowds have gone home
and the janitor, pushes the big mustache of his broom across the floor,
and I ask, "Dad, is that you in there?"

"No, it's not."

A black cloud in the shape of Magritte's bowler,
plump and slick and sleek and stark, hanging over the train station, says,
"I want to go to a museum; put one in the poem beside the station."

where it's morning and the ticket window is selling
tickets to a man in a hat and an enormous
trench coat, wrinkled and jowly, a woman

in white looks as cool as a martini in a chrome
shaker, a woman in red seethes in a doorway,
eager to become one of Those Beginning the Journey
and from the horizon' molten light, the trains crawl out.

"And when I get to the museum I want to see
Soutine, Miro, Picasso, or Dali, I want eyes in my armpits
and my fingers, eyes in the air, the trees, the dirt."

"Father," I say, "you already are an eye-in-the-dirt."

It's early morning. In the pine tree I hear the phoebe's stressed
squeak, *fee-bee, fee-bay,* like the creak of the old guard at the museum
snoozing in his rocker before Soutine's still life of the butchered cows.

"Father," I say, "do you see them?"
And the phoebe says, Yes-squeak—yes-squeak-yes-squeak-yes-squeak.

The Burial

After I've goosed up the fire in the stove with *Starter Logg*
so that it burns like fire on amphetamines, after it's imprisoned,
screaming and thrashing, behind the stove door; after I've
listened to the dead composers and watched the brown-plus-gray
deer compose into Cubism the trees whose name I don't know;
after I've holed up in my loneliness staring
at the young buck whose two new antlers are like a snail's
stalked eyes and I've let this conceit lead me to the eyes-on-stems
of the faces of Picasso and from there to my dead father; after I've
chased the deer away (they were boring, streamlined machines
for tearing up green things, deer are the cows-of-the-forest);
then I bend down over the sea of keys to write this poem
about my father in his grave.

It isn't easy. It's dark in my room, the door is closed,
all around is creaking and sighing, as though I were in the hold
of a big ship, as though I were in the dark sleep
of a huge freighter toiling across the landscape of the waves
taking me to my father with whom I have struggled
like Jacob with the angel and who heaves off, one final time,
the muddy counterpane of the earth and lies panting
beside his grave like a large dog who has run a long way.

This is as far as he goes. I stand at the very end
of myself holding a shovel. The blade is long and cool;
it is an instrument for organizing the world; the blade is
drenched in shine, the air is alive along it, as air is alive
on the windshield of a car. Beside me my father droops
as though he were under anesthesia. He is so thin,
and he doesn't have a coat. My left hand grows
cool and sedate under the influence of his flesh.
It hesitates and then . . .

My father drops in like baggage into a hold.
I close the hinged lid, and above him I heap a
firmament of dirt. The body alone, in the dark,
in the cold, without a coat. I would not wish that on my
greatest enemy. Which, in a sense, my father was.

These Days,

in the teary windows, the woodlands heave
and twitch, and my neighbor, in her dark parka,
looks like a nail hammered into the fat upholstery
of the drifts. The silence clinks and clanks,
and my father's here as the endless task
that trickles down from the muse's mills
and shops. I have been bad. *Get back
in the grave, for god's sake, Father!* I tell him.
And he tells me, *I hate this poem about the fire.*

I never write from experience,
but halfway through the poem the fire bit me.
Just as I was feeding it the log that looks
like an autopsy performed on a telephone
pole, the fire turned on me like a sick dog.
Bitch. Bastard. What's fire's gender?
Bachelard says fire is the daughter of two
logs. Okay, so I am writing a poem in
which I am peering down the long dark
road of a sentence and I hear my father saying
*I knew a woman whose mind was like a
white veranda across which her thoughts
could glide in brilliant congress with one
another. Who are you dating?*

The log I've named Gretel wells up dully,
her hair is a yellow fire struggling.
When it comes to Gretel, I am God.
I love the lush brocade of gray and black
the fire makes upon the logs. I am in favor
of the well-dressed. My dad looked great
buried in his tweeds from the Denver Junior
League. The snow, in drifts and bulging
hunks, reminds me of the casket's satin lining.

They snowplowed the dirt down on him.
I heard the roar of earth falling on the coffin.
I am pushing my luck with the stove. I just fed it a log
big enough to choke a horse. Even fire needs
a challenge. These days, the disappearance of matter
is what interests me most.

Talking with Frank O'Hara

"Frank," I say,

"the dead, those doorstops, are fine by me,"
 and I turn the gas so low my poem almost gutters out.

 Still, in the landscape,
 a red flame glints—

 a fleck of flesh.

"But poetry is zippy," Frank exclaims.
"What is it with you

 and the downbeat?"

 We are staring at the sunset
 bulging against the window.

 And at the crows.
 We love the crows—

 the dark snout of them among the trees.
 So ungainly, so light, they are scattered

 all over the yard, clinkers. Cold coals.
 Here, poetry is not too easy

 as most things are
 the dull particulars of Mirror Street

 one beside the other.
 We drink and smoke.

 I quote Frank to Frank: "I miss myself," I say,

because this morning, pawing through his poems,
Manhattan came back to me like a heart attack.

I miss that saturnine, bookish, sexy,
fragment of a bedroom on West 10th

its windows filled with the maple's
leafy reach, the creak and lurch of swings, the bicyclettes.

I was so intelligent and lonely
stuck up there under the dark eaves of my mind . . .

"And what," I demand, "happened to those years of art and sorrow?
To the misfortunes of Kline, and Pollock, and Peter Beck

and the man who whispered in the keyhole
'Frank is dead'

and the way half New York sank down and wept?"

A flock of crows reels past, cindery and remote.
"Poetry is a bat out of hell," says Frank.

Metamorphosis

"What's happened to me? he thought

—Franz Kafka

As for myself—wherever there was a street going indifferently about her business,
I was the dog.
At first I wept.
I became its beatings, shitting on command, bred and bred into more and more of it.
I crouched behind its bark, still as a stone ax.
I lunged at a greasy picnic on the table of some lawn.
I was dog's belonging, dog told me. We were nothing in and of ourselves—
      one fiction abusing another.
I woke up in the cave of its crate, in the kennel of its name, the hinges of our jaws
      locked tight by the muzzle.
My nose became an organ of thoughtfulness, my ears were shells in which the seas
      of the voices of the world thrashed and
Night fell, day rose, the old died, the young went on.
One night I lay down and in the morning I was dog and my actions were fetched
      by orders: *fetch, lie down, lie down here.*
Shaggy mat of stinks. The tide of thought receded. I howled at the door
      of my own mind wanting out of that empty house.
And the voices of the masters perched above me said, *you are just a gregarious*
      piece of furniture.
The war came and went beyond the bars of my life. I was dog.
Then I embraced it.
Then I was undone and replaced it.

Stray Dogg

(Nameless street, sounds of traffic and panting. Dogg is lost.)

i wuz followin a boot
down the avenew,

the smell uf wet meat clung to it.

i wuz leapen over ashes an trashes
wit out a license

runnin frum the p'lease—the gas, net, an boot.

This iz the life, i thot–
a planet uf ruin an disorder

an the doggs uf the world
runnin the world.

From the doorway waggs
the long smell uf coffee

"We haf gone to the dawgs,"
i heard sum one sayin.

There wuz a door open
i went into it.

Dogg Howse

(Dogg has a day.)

They tolt me each dogg has its door.
i walkt up to this one.

i gnaw on the shues. i try on the howls.
It wuz rainin, it wuz snowin

upon the narrow howses.
i bark at the untertakers,

an at the mellencollie howl uf the frates,
an at the mellencollie howl uf the frates.

Mistrust,
i am wearee uf the struggle not to bee dogg
as iron filings must be wearee uf the magnut.

But now i am yr dogg.
i will bee dawg uf the yard!

Leapin frantic an dootifull
like a pubblick fountin,
like a piston rammin against the howsin—

leapin iz my steddee job.

Hang Dogg

(A court room. Dogg is arrested and on trial.)

The court askt,

wuz i guiltee uf "Indigence?
Derangement? Identitee? Gender?"

Wuz i "in the abstract or particular,
A bitch? A witch? A lush?"

"R yew now or haf yew been
Medicated? Evicted? Wasted?"

Wuz i Mexican?
Engleash speaker?

guiltee uf pezzimizm?

"An where wuz yew on the nite in qwestion?"

The court askt,

Wuz it my fault the Warr wuz lost?
Wuz i not the Dogg uf Warr?

If not
whut kind uf dogg?

"How many fingers iz we holdin up?"

"R yew guiltee uf crossin the border? R yew a boarder?
How much monee dew yew haf in yr pockets?

Where r yr pockets?

R yew that dogg
the countree iz goin to?

Iz that yew?

They sd: Dogg
Yew iz toast.

Who Iz Dogg?

(At the pound, Dogg is interrogated.)

Who iz that scrawnee filth?
they askt Dogg.

Who iz that pack
that runs togedder?

Who iz that racket uf instinct in the brane?
Ribs stickin out like bucket staves?

Who iz those howls? Who iz standin-at-the-post-in-chains
an puts itself between us an our rage?

Who iz bearin-the-beatin
iz drownt, burnt, flayt?

Who iz gnashs-at-the-gate,
who iz haunts-us-thru-the-swamp?

Who sides wit the p'lease against us?
Who drags us back

to our fetters?
Against whom duz that pack slash back?

Who iz yew? they askt.
And Dogg sd—yew iz.

Dead Dogg

That the Dogges be killed by the Dogge-killers appointed
—Order, Lord Mayor, Concerning the Plague

Fateful Dogg took 2,000 volts

strove to hold the juice,
monstrously heaped upon it, stone by stone,

hovered in the fog of shocks
cowered in the field of barks

then stepped aside to watch
the glues of the heart loosen and give up.

Within the heaven of death
Fateful Dogge went *ruff*

because the words jostled so far off
shore, so not-here, so—*Whut?*

The words for words failed Dogg.

V

The Angels of the Resurrection

Even when it's become a piece of furniture
upholstered in the stiff brocade of rigor mortis,
a corpse blistered with acids into a tapestry,
poked full of holes by bullets, and blurred
by miles of roads, they find it.
They find the body because
there is no where it can go, there is no death
deep or dark enough, no unlit alley bleak enough to hide it.
Even hidden it brings the resurrection to it,
even lying low in the slot of the unmarked grave,
its carnality works like a magnet.
They will find it, haul it leaking and weeping
up from the black suction of the fathomless lake.
The lakes, the woods, the gardens are filled
with its unmentionable perfumes.
The body cannot hide, and there's no room
for modesty, no provision for rest.
They are dogs and wolves. They will find it.
They will dig it up.

The Dig

Beyond the dark souks of the old city, beyond the Dome of the Rock
gray and humped and haunted, beyond the eyes of the men at the café
where they drink their thimblesful of hot tea, beyond the valley
with its scar of naked pipe, the perfect geometrical arcs of irrigation,
and someone incising a dark furrow in a field, some plowman's black
gutter opening through the green, she is waist deep in this open grave,
staring at the delicate puzzle of my feet. Beyond her, in the shadow
of Tel el-Hesi, daubing and dampening the earth, another woman finds
the faint brickwork of floor spidering the dust, on the hearth's
wedge-shaped arc of shadow, a scattering of charred millet.
Nothing else for miles. Nothing but this bluff of ruin,
one decapitated tower, one "window" staved into the brick,
the bougainvillea crawling across a wall dragging its little bloody rags.
She is standing here thinking she cannot bear the way this foot—
my foot—wants to step out of the earth. I don't care. I am using her
to leave the grave. And so we go on. We go on until we cannot go on
deepening my grave, and the trowel hits stone and I lie staring
while she makes the earth recede, reaches in and pulls me out,
my jaw wired shut by roots, my skull so full of dirt that suddenly
the intricate sutures come loose and, in her hands, the whole head opens.
In the shallow setting where I lay is the small triangular sail
of a scapula, the ribs like the grill of a car. She bones me like a fish.
She lays the little pieces, the puzzling odds and ends, into the dishes
of shellac and formalin. One carpal still wears the faint blue
stain of a ring. Wearily, I lean my reassembled head,
sutures rich with glue, against the wall of the filled beaker.
A fine sweat of bubbles on my chin. All night, through the window
of my jar, I watch her mend with glue and wire, the shallow
saucer of my pelvis. We are nothing. Earth staring at earth.

The Murder Writer

The living teetered at the edge of a cliff.
Below the living lies the lake, that slick, black
plate of water, and just behind them purred

a car as dark and hollow as a hearse.
I dipped my pen into that inky place.
The cloudy brow of night

was furrowed in concern,
because the living did not seem to know
that they were being stalked by me.

Night after night I tried to nudge them
into the water, the path of a train,
or my oncoming speed.

But they were always busy:
The woman in red waxed
and waned, smoldered like a mine fire

just beneath the surface of the page.
And the woman in white was always
asleep inside the simple moonbeam of herself.

The car was ready, and the cliff;
the moon was a drop of mercury
that rolled back and forth across

the night, and beside the black
vat of reservoir I had planted witnesses
like flowers in the rubber pots of their galoshes.

I sat and smoked and lingered.
Inside me a murder sulked and ached
like a lake behind a dam.

I was waiting until the world was on my side
and would turn itself murderous for my sake.

Dead Girl's Bedroom

                                        Someone's stuffed the lilies
into the choke hold of the vase.   The limp hand of a white glove
                      tries to crawl from the coffin of a drawer.
This shot's tired. No, exhausted. The whole room
has the soft stillness of a dead kitten.
We seem to move from shot to shot like someone changing dresses.
Dying is   a wealth of contradictions.
Living's for hicks, the room asserts. These days, nobody
but nobody *lives*.

Soliloquy of the Depressed Book

Since I have come to hate Nature & its Poetry,
I hate every landscape pinned down by Scenery—
The Mountain Package, The Garden, The Vista
always flapping in my face;
I can't pour my broken heart into those rented rooms
with their tired aquatinted distances.
Don't be viewy, I think,
& soap shut the blue window of the sky.
I want machinery
to grind the mountains down to Mountain,
to drive the trees, like stakes, through the heart of The Glade.
I want images to inherit the earth
like kudzu spreading its ooze,
its mean replications, its malignant increase
over the landscape,
erasing the boundaries between itself & us,
between show & tell, master & slave,
until The World vanishes,
& we are left with an Image of The World.
Now every pane of glass in every window
is stenciled with images, even the doorknob,
like a tiny goldfish bowl,
is aswarm with them.
Every avenue of escape is closed.
Stop, say the red stop signs
that once were cardinals.
The wet & bloody pulp that once was Sunset seethes.
Night drags its glassy, abstract fingers
over the glassy abstract harp of Wind.
The World & I vanish into a dark
Image of The World-in-Darkness
which I remember was once merely
a mote in my own eye, a distant lark,
night on the dull horizon—
coming to serve me.

. . .

April 18, the 21st Century

Cher Baudelaire,

Tonight as I boarded my train of thought and entered the first class compartment of my mind, I thought of Margaret Atwood who wrote, "I am in love with Raymond Chandler because of his interest in furniture." Baudelaire, I am no one but the insatiable identities that descend upon me, and tonight it is you. I've thought, "if Baudelaire were not Baudelaire, I would be Baudelaire," though, in truth, I have thought the same about Walter Benjamin when he says (I paraphrase), "I am in love with Baudelaire because of his interest in furniture. When writing about furniture Baudelaire is free from capitalism's philosophy and history and archeology and is enthralled by upholstery, and this is a way of thinking and being that is wholly new in the world and was made so by Baudelaire."

No quotation is innocent. Every quotation is an act of ventriloquism. Every ventriloquism is a usurpation. As R. P. Blackmur said (and here I do not quote but paraphrase): "If you say there is no blackbird in a poem, immediately a blackbird alights on the branch of a line." If you say, "I am only quoting," immediately your voice guiltily alights on the branches of the words.

In *Charles Baudelaire: A Lyric Poet in the Era of High Capitalism*, as Walter Benjamin carries forward the great cross of his love for you, at the height of his passion, he stops on page seventy-one to quote that gnat Maxime Du Camp:

Baudelaire had what is a great defect in a writer, a defect of which he was not aware: he was ignorant. . . . He remained unacquainted with history, physiology, archeology and philosophy. . . . He had little interest in the outside world; he may have been aware of it, but he certainly did not study it.

And in doing so, at the height of his love, Walter Benjamin enters and is entered and becomes Maxime Du Camp. "Baudelaire knew nothing," says (sneers) Benjamin. Why, I have always wondered, does he do that?

Cher Baudelaire, I believe that behind or inside Benjamin's quotation from Maxine Du Camp, growing upon it as a vine grows on a trellis, there lives the envy and sorrow of a man cut off from the possibility of another's experience. There lives the envy of a man who knew history for another man who did not. There lives the love of a man (Benjamin) who loved philosophy for a man (you) who did not. By extension, therefore, you would not have loved Benjamin or perhaps you could not love him. Would you have wasted an afternoon on Benjamin? No. Is there even one syllable in you to suggest that you care at all about Benjamin? No. Which must have hurt.

I, on the other hand, am perfectly aware that you adore me because we adore so many of the same things—furniture, women's dresses, recreational drugs. In every line and flourish I hear you calling out to me as I sit here in the furnishings of the future. I see you waving to me in the windows of my train of thought as though you were waving to yourself at some time in the future; as though I were you with my poems filled with dresses and drugs and unfaithful women, some of whom are me. How grateful you are that I have resurrected you, that you can live in the present with all its wonderful appurtenances, with its fantastic advances in perfumes, the advent of hair gel, the Alps of the four-inch stiletto. How lucky you are, cher Baudelaire, to have found me to shelter you, to have found the succulent hallways of my lines, and the shimmering windows of my tropes, and the sticky navels of the little hash pipes I have left lying about for you, the ease, the comfort, the respite my verse provides you.

Or maybe not. I sit on my train and watch capitalism struggle in the windows. In the city of the mind the great alcove of night closes over us. Even over you, Baudelaire, who invented a world that had never before existed—a completely interior world without philosophy—and in so doing gained the undying envy of the future Walter Benjamin, who was sentenced to live inside a world outside and who, therefore, had to save himself from that world and its history by committing suicide at Hotel de Francia in Port-Bou in September of 1940.

Homage to Dickinson

I've never longed for the annulments of Heaven,
nor for Hell, that orgy of repenting,
but have wanted the loneliness of this
slender room and bed, the cool neatness
of being dead: to be reduced, cleaned out,
a manageable mess, nothing left but knobs
and buttons, the skull an empty crock,
the pelvis a washed plate, the ribs laid
tidily, side by side. And I would be gone,
not that stern white dress, not that thing
with the Bible on her breasts. I would be
nothing but one narrow room of sepulcher,
one barred window where traffic never brings
its soot, the ear clean and empty as a scrubbed cup,
the tongue at rest and I, free at last, the window
of myself cast open, and all the sweet lament
of mourners throbbing in the distance, the angels'
white blouses pinned to the line of the horizon.
I would be alone, alone, in my maidenly
tomb, my own woman. Finally. And forever.

Like God,

you hover above the page staring down
on a small town. Outside a window
some scenery loafs in a sleepy hammock
of pastoral prose and here is a mongrel
loping and here is a train approaching
the station in three long sentences and
here are the people in galoshes waiting.
But you know this story about the galoshes
is really About Your Life, so, like a diver
climbing over the side of a boat and down
into the ocean, you climb, sentence
by sentence, into this story on this page.

You have been expecting yourself
as a woman who purrs by in a dress
by Patou, and a porter manacled to
the luggage, and a man stalking across
the page like a black cloud in a bad mood.
These are your fellow travelers and
you are a face behind or inside these
faces, a heartbeat in the volley of these
heartbeats, as you choose, out of all
the journeys, the journey of a man
with a mustache, scented faintly with
Prince Albert. "He must be a secret
sensualist," you think and your awareness
drifts to his trench coat, worn, softened,
and flabby, just as the train pulls into the station.

No, you would prefer another stop
in a later chapter where the climate is
affable and sleek. But the passengers
are disembarking, and you did not
choose to be in the story of the woman

in the white dress which is as cool and
evil as a glass of radioactive milk. You
did not choose to be in the story of the
matron whose bosom is like the prow
of a ship and who is launched toward
lunch at the Hotel Pierre, or even the
story of the dog-on-a-leash, even though
this is now your story: the story of the
person-who-had-to-take-the-train-and-walk-
the-dark-road described hurriedly by
someone sitting at the tavern so you could
discover it, although you knew all along
the road would be there, you, who have
been hovering above this page, holding
the book in your hands, like God, reading.

Then, Suddenly—

Yes, in the distance there is a river, a bridge,
there is a sun smeared to a rosy blur, red as
a drop of blood on a slide. Under this sun,
droves of poetry readers saunter home
almost unaware that they are unemployed.
I'm tired of the dark forest of this book
and the little trail of bread crumbs I have
to leave so readers who say *garsh* a lot
can get the hang of it and follow along.
And so I begin to erase the forest and
the trees because trees depress me, even
the idea of a tree depresses me. I also
erase the white aster of a street lamp's
drooping face; I erase a dog named Arf;
I erase four cowboys in bolas and yet in
the diminishing bustle of these streets I
nevertheless keep meeting People-I-Know.
I erase them. Now I am surrounded by
the faces of strangers which I also erase
until there is only scenery. I hate scenery.
I wind rivers back on their spools, I unplug
the bee from the socket of the honeysuckle
and the four Black Angus that just walked in
like a string quartet. "Get a life," I tell them.
"Get a life in another world, because this is
a page as bare and smooth as a bowling alley,"
and, then, suddenly—renouncing all matter—
I am gone, and all that's left is a voice, soaring,
invisible, disembodied, gobbling up the landscape,
a cloud giving a poetry reading
at which, Reader, I have made our paths cross!

Acknowledgments

Below, in alphabetical order, is a list of the poems reprinted from my previous books. A few of these poems have been edited from the version that first appeared in print.

The poems "Starlet in Satin Dressing Gown" and "The Garden" were recently published in the *American Poetry Review*. "Angels of the Resurrection" was carved out of a much longer prose poem that also recently appeared in the *American Poetry Review*. "Lunch Break with Ted Berrigan and Neighbor's House on Fire" and "Self-Portrait as Items in a Snowy Lithograph" appeared this past year in the *Boston Review*. The poems "Talking with Frank O'Hara", "Dead Girl's Bedroom", and "Dead Dogg" are published here for the first time.

Many people have read and commented on these poems over the years, but, for their extreme tenacity and patience, thank you to Maggie Anderson, Deborah Bogen, the late Patricia Dobler, Molly Peacock, Jeffrey Schwartz, and Judith Vollmer. My unending gratitude to Civitella Ranieri. And yet again, thank you, Ed.

Hotel Fiesta. Athens, Georgia: University of Georgia Press, 1984.

> "Frying Trout While Drunk"
> "Kiss"
> "Of Your Father's Indiscretions and the Train to California"
> "Ordinary Objects"
> "Self-Portrait"
> "She Is Six"
> "The Sleeping"
> "When Father Decided He Did Not Love Her Anymore"

The Dig. The National Poetry Series. Urbana and Chicago: University of Illinois Press, 1992.

> "A Poem Like An Automobile Can Take You Anywhere"
> "Big Black Car"
> "Blonde Bombshell"
> "The Dig"
> "Drawing Rosie's Train Trip"

"Dying Was" (as "What Dying Was")
"Grieving Was" (as "What Grieving Was")
"Heartsick"
"Homage to Dickinson"
"Inspiration"
"On Waking after Dreaming of Raoul"
"Outside Room Six"
"The Past"
"The Planet Krypton"
"Seizure"
"Self-Portrait at Eighteen"
"Spite—Homage to Sylvia Plath"
"Stone Soup"
"The Technology of Love"
"Walt, I Salute You!"

Then, Suddenly—. Pittsburgh: University of Pittsburgh Press, 1999.

"The Burial"
"Dressing the Parts"
"Halfway Through the Book I'm Writing"
"Homage to Sharon Stone"
"In English in a Poem"
"inside gertrude stein"
"Like God,"
"Out of Metropolis"
"The Politics of Narrative: Why I Am a Poet"
"Portrait of the Author"
"Soliloquy of the Depressed Book"
"Then, Suddenly—"
"These Days"
"The White Dress"

Noose and Hook. Pittsburgh: University of Pittsburgh Press, 2010.

"April 18th, the 21st Century"
"Ars Poetica" (as "Personal experiences are chains and balls")
"Dogg House"
"Hang Dogg"
"Hello, Mallarme"
"Into the clearing of . . ."
"I tried to flatter myself into extinction"
"Metamorphosis"
"The Murder Writer" (as "The living teetered at the edge . . .)
"The Occupation"
"Stray Dogg"
"While my mother lies in a hospital bed . . ."
"Who Iz Dogg?"

10/15